# Houghton Mifflin Harcourt
# Physics

# Engineering Design Guide

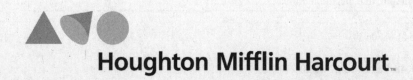

Houghton Mifflin Harcourt

# Contents

## Physics Engineering Design Guide

# Lesson 1: What Is Engineering?

Engineering and science are closely related, and in fact, engineers and scientists often work together to solve problems of interest to both. Despite their close connection, however, the two fields have distinct goals. *Engineering* applies scientific principles to design and build products and processes that are useful to humankind. *Science* is the system of knowledge humans have about the physical world and its phenomena, based on observation and experimentation. Put less formally, science is a way to study the natural world, whereas engineering is a way to achieve practical solutions.

Both science and engineering rely on evidence and follow a structured investigative process that may involve data, mathematics, models, and computational thinking. Both fields involve asking questions and solving problems. Scientific investigations generally ask questions to develop explanations for phenomena. Engineering studies ask questions to help define a specific problem and find a solution. Both science and engineering are interrelated with technology.

## Technology

In its broadest sense, *technology* is the application of scientific knowledge for practical purposes. Technology is a process as well as the goods, services, and products that result from that process. Some of the earliest technology included the use of simple stone tools to do work and two-wheeled carts to move goods and humans. Today, many goods are mass-produced in vast factories utilizing complex machinery controlled by computerized systems; similar systems control the transport of those goods across the globe. Technology, then, can be said to include all human-designed and human-produced solutions and tools.

Modern technology touches virtually every aspect of the human environment, from agriculture and manufacturing to computer science and the aerospace industry. Viewed that way, technology can seem like something that involves only "big things." Yet technology touches every part of your life every day. Look around your classroom. Just about everything you see is the result of technology. The notebook on your desk, the pencil in your hand, the shoes on your feet, the cell phone in your pocket, the water bottle and snack bar in your backpack—even the backpack itself—were all designed by engineers and produced using technology. Without technology, life would be very different indeed.

## Types of Engineering

Engineering is a large and complex field composed of many branches and subspecialties that in turn serve many industries. Here are some examples of the types of engineers.

- Mechanical engineers design engines as well as all kinds of other machines: from cars and robotics to toys and roller coasters.

- Electrical engineers work in a wide range of fields, from power companies to defense contractors. They also design software and develop consumer electronics, such as smart phones and televisions.

- Closely related to electrical engineering is computer engineering, which helps develop computers, computer-based solutions for a range of industries, and of course, computer games.

- Chemical engineering serves a diverse array of industries, from large-scale production of industrial chemicals to pharmaceuticals. Chemical engineers also may work closely with environmental agencies to find solutions for recycling and similar problems.

- Civil engineers are critical to public works projects, such as building bridges, highways, and dams. Some civil engineers find ways to bring clean water to the public.

- Various engineering subfields in the life sciences involve solutions for producing food, pharmaceuticals, and biofuels, as well as protecting the environment.

## The Connection Among Science, Technology, and Engineering

Science and engineering are closely interconnected with technology. The work of scientists brings knowledge that engineers draw on when designing solutions to solve a problem or meet a practical need. These solutions may then drive advances in technology that enable further scientific investigations. For example, the early achievements of scientists working with electricity led engineers to create power grids that brought electricity to homes, businesses, and public areas across the world.

The work of engineers, in turn, creates technologies such as microscopes, measuring instruments, and imaging software that scientists rely on to do work and conduct research. The development of the Hubble Space Telescope made it possible for astronomers to expand our knowledge of Earth's place in the universe, and brought insight into the origins of stars and galaxies. The James Webb Space Telescope will extend this reach into the universe. Even development of a seemingly humble instrument, such as a digital electronic balance or dissolved oxygen meter, can improve precision in measurements, allowing scientists to achieve more accurate results in lab work.

New ideas gleaned from science often bring a need for new technologies. These technologies, in turn, are developed by engineers and then utilized by scientists for further scientific investigations. The interconnectedness among scientific inquiry, engineering design, and technological development is reflected in the key roles each plays through the cycle of research and development.

## The Impact of Science, Engineering, and Technology on Society

The interrelatedness of scientific knowledge, engineering solutions, and technological advances has had a profound and lasting effect on human society and the natural environment. For example, insights from scientific investigations have altered the way bridges are designed, crops are raised, surgery is performed, and machinery is produced.

Human society, in turn, influences science and engineering through its goals and expectations for technological developments. A range of economic, cultural, and political factors may drive decisions for improving or replacing technologies. Society also sets limits on the work of scientists and engineers, such as regulating the extraction of resources or in establishing acceptable levels of pollution from mining, farming, and industry.

# A World of Engineering

Imagine a construction material that absorbs and destroys smog. Picture a robot that carries a patient and provides for other healthcare needs and comfort. Think about how solar panels built into roads could revolutionize highway travel. Engineers turn these and countless other ideas into reality. Those are just a few ways in which engineers use their science and math skills, and their creativity, to develop technologies for today and tomorrow.

# Engineering and Physics

A foundation in physics is critical in almost every field of engineering, from designing toys to bridges to spacecraft. A few areas of engineering that are closely integrated with physics are described below. These and other engineering specialties are discussed in more detail in Lesson 2.

## Lesson 1: What Is Engineering? *continued*

Two familiar areas of engineering are mechanical engineering and civil engineering. Mechanical engineers design and build machines, from automobiles and skateboards to robots and turbines, using their knowledge of force, motion, heat transfer, fluid mechanics, and more to build safe, durable products. They often work closely with engineers in other disciplines to solve problems; for example, mechanical engineers might work with environmental and electrical engineers to design and build solar panels and wind turbines.

Like mechanical engineers, civil engineers are builders of things both great and small. Civil engineers use their knowledge of physics, specifically classical mechanics (force, motion, energy, and work), to design and build structures such as dams, levees, and bridges. Many civil engineers also have a foundation in geophysics, which integrates knowledge of geology and physics, providing the knowledge needed to evaluate the capacity of soil and rocks to bear heavy loads, and most effective ways to improve irrigation and flood-control systems.

Aircraft, spacecraft, and satellites are just some of the concerns of aerospace engineers. Knowledge of force and motion (specifically propulsion) and how trajectories and the laws of gravity work all are essential tools for these professionals. Aerospace engineers who develop avionics—the electronic and communications systems used on aircraft and spacecraft—also need to understand how electrical systems work.

Electrical engineering is a broad field that requires a strong knowledge of electricity and magnetism. Electrical engineers who design machines, electronic products, and communication systems need a thorough understanding not only of electric circuits, but also power and magnetism. Electrical engineers who design software and computer games must also be well grounded in knowledge of computers and programming.

## Questions

1. How might the interrelatedness of science, engineering, and technology drive the development of a new type of light bulb?

2. Briefly describe the impact that development of a new technique to mine copper might have on society, and how society might in turn have an impact on further development of similar technology.

# Lesson 2: Engineering, Physics, and Robots

## A Robotic Challenge

The United States Defense Advanced Research Projects Agency, known as DARPA, is a government agency that oversees research and development programs in the scientific and engineering community. This agency is always looking for new challenges and their potential solutions. The DARPA Robotics Challenge was a competition to develop new robotics technology that could be used in case of natural and human-made disasters. Some of the most advanced robotics research and development organizations in the world worked furiously to develop the hardware, software, sensors, and controls that would make up their robots. Beginning in 2013, teams consisting of engineers, computer experts, and robots began the demanding competition. There were two trials and a final competition over a two-year period. During that time, the teams learned what would be expected from their robots.

DARPA launched the project as a response to a need for rescue robots. Although the human body has often been compared to a machine, it has limitations. These limits became clear in March of 2011, when a devastating earthquake and tsunami badly damaged a nuclear power plant in Fukushima, Japan. Equipment failed, resulting in explosions and the release of large amounts of radiation. Humans could not enter the plant to try to limit the damage; it was too dangerous.

The goal of the DARPA competition was to speed up the development of rescue robots that could enter areas too dangerous for humans and perform tasks to reduce the impact of these disasters. Ultimately, the robots had to perform eight tasks that would be relevant to disaster response, such as driving a vehicle alone, walking through rubble, tripping circuit breakers, turning valves, opening doors, and climbing stairs.

Most robots today function only in carefully controlled factories or research lab environments, and they perform simple tasks over and over. They cannot function in an unpredictable disaster zone because humans must control their every move. The DARPA competition required that the rescue robots be capable of maneuvering in environments they had never encountered. They would have to use tools that were designed for humans without being reprogrammed. This meant that when the operator commanded the robot to close a valve, the robot would be able to identify the valve, apply the correct force to the valve, and maneuver its limbs appropriately so that the valve turned in the correct direction with no further programming.

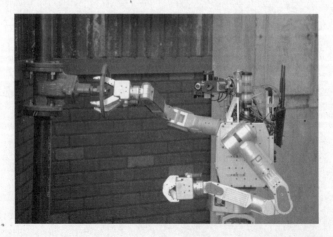

## Mechanical Engineering

A mechanical engineer designs the mechanical components of the robot's structure: how its joint mechanisms will function, the type of bearings it will have, and its heat characteristics. The engineer may also work on the robot's sensors. After the robot is designed, the engineer is involved in building and maintaining it. He or she might also find new applications for the robot. For example, a robot that is designed to pilot itself on other planets might be adaptable as a self-piloting crop harvester. A robot that is built to assemble small electrical devices might be able to disable explosives. The use of robots in agriculture, mining, and nuclear power plant maintenance is growing rapidly as engineers think creatively about what robots can do.

One of the first decisions a mechanical engineer must make when starting to design a robot is what material it should be made of. Many robots are made of metal because it is strong. An engineer's knowledge of materials science is very important in making this decision.

If a robot is to move, the engineer must decide what components will allow that movement. For example, should the robot be bipedal (two limbs), quadrupedal (four limbs), or hexapedal (six limbs)? Bipedal robots usually are easier to control and are more stable and energy efficient. They move quickly and can travel over rough terrain without falling over. But not all robots are designed to be mobile. Some stay in one place and do their job.

Mechanical engineers on the DARPA Robotics Challenge teams had many decisions to make. What would be the overall structure of the robot? Most of the teams decided early on to use a human shape, but how would it operate? Would it have limbs or would it roll? If limbs, how many? Would it have "feet" or would it have treads? Having treads makes walking on rubble easier, but having feet makes stair climbing easier. Some of the competing robots had "fingers," but others did not. How well a robot performs a simple task like turning a door handle depends on this choice. Turning a valve might be easier with a different design. Designing a robot that can do both is an engineering challenge.

As the robots took shape, the engineers made many changes. For example, the winning team from the Republic of Korea decided after the first trial that wheels on their robot's "knees" would improve its ability to kneel down and move through small openings. They added small wheels, and the robot's performance improved—so much so that it won the first prize of $2 million!

## Electrical and Computer Engineering

Electrical and computer engineering are at the heart of modern robots. While mechanical engineers are responsible for a robot's external structure, electrical and computer engineers bring the robot to life, making it more than just an assortment of metal and plastic parts.

Electrical and computer engineers develop networks of sensors that allow their robots to function. Sensors provide information about a robot's surroundings. Vision sensors are well advanced today, due in part to the technology developed for cell-phone cameras. More development is needed for other kinds of sensors, such as flexible, tactile skin sensors, brain-wave sensors, and force sensors.

Sensors pass on information to actuators that operate the robot. An actuator is a mechanism, similar to a motor, for activating process control equipment using pneumatic, hydraulic, or electronic signals. Both sensors and actuators are designed by electrical and computer engineers. For example, a robotic arm may need several types of actuators depending on the tasks it must perform. Research areas for actuator design include fingered hands, tentacles, bouncy wheels, legs, and surgical instruments.

In the DARPA competition, one task involved cutting a hole in a wall. The vision, motion, and force sensors had to provide enough detailed information for the robot to perform this task.

## Software Engineering

The best-designed and best-built robot will not be able to function on its own if its behavior is not programmed into its electronic parts. This is the job of a software engineer. The computer software provides the link between the sensors and the actuators that control the robot's movements. The sensors see a door handle or a valve, and then the software has to recognize what the sensors saw and give the arms and hands the directions to open the door or turn the valve. Similarly, when the sensors see rough terrain, the software has to judge where the obstacles are and maneuver the legs and feet to get over those obstacles without falling.

Most robots have programs that allow them to perform a few tasks in a limited place. If you move the robot to a new environment, it may not be able to adapt and perform its tasks. Many of the robots in the DARPA competition did not have adaptable software. Human operators had to see what the sensors saw and provide the instructions to the robot about what to do. One of the goals in software development is to produce software that can adapt to new stimuli just as humans do. Sensing, planning, control, reasoning, and learning are all humanlike capabilities that software engineers are trying to reproduce in a computer-based robotic system.

| Lesson 2: Engineering, Physics, and Robots *continued*

# Mechatronics

Mechatronics is a multidisciplinary field of engineering that combines systems engineering, mechanical engineering, electrical engineering, telecommunications engineering, control engineering, and computer engineering. The word *mechatronics* is a combination of the word *mechanisms,* meaning "machines that move," and *electronics*. Mechatronics describes robotics perfectly because it integrates electrical and mechanical systems in a single device. Mechatronics has also been described as the addition of intelligence to a mechanical design or replacing a mechanical design with an intelligent electronic solution. This does not mean that robots can think. Rather, it means that computer science and design must be involved in making a robot work. A robot is an example of a mechatronic system.

The field of mechatronics grew out of early robotics in the 1960s. Early robotic arms were unable to coordinate their movements without sensory feedback, so input from other disciplines was needed. Other early applications of mechatronics were designing technology for products such as automatic door openers, vending machines, and antilock brakes. The addition of kinematic and high-level programming changed the robotics field. Engineers also improved performance by embedding microprocessors in their designs. After that, computational intelligence was added to mechatronics and robot design.

Modern robots may be any shape and size, but all are preprogrammed and interact physically with the world. To create a robot, an engineer typically employs kinematics to determine the robot's range of motion and mechanics to determine the stresses within the robot. Today's robots explore the Martian surface, the ocean floor, and disaster sites. The next generation of robots that will approach human intelligence in their capabilities will need to incorporate ultrafast image processing. Industrial designers will be charged with making the robots' outsides attractive and the insides work well together. More and more, robots will become an important part of modern life.

# Questions

1. An engineering team has been asked to design and build a robotic hand. What tasks might a mechanical, an electrical, and a software engineer be in charge of?

2. What types of sensors would a robot need to drive a car? What kind of engineer would be most likely to design these sensors?

3. Other than the example given in the text, describe a scenario in which a rescue robot might be valuable.

# Lesson 3: Engineering Design Process

Engineers typically follow a design process to develop the best solutions to problems. This lesson describes that process. You'll discover that the steps in the process can be used to design solutions to problems in your everyday life, such as preparing food or planning a trip, as well as larger problems, such as adding lights to your school's grounds. In the activities that follow this lesson, you'll have the opportunity to apply the design process to several engineering problems.

Like scientific inquiry, engineering design is a process based on a set of practices that can be used in flexible ways. In general, you can think of the engineering design process as having three main phases:

- **Define and Delimit the Problem** Clearly state the problem, describe the characteristics of a successful solution, and identify any factors that limit the solution.

- **Design Solutions** Generate ideas for possible solutions; select and test the most promising design solution.

- **Optimize Solutions** Use the results of testing to refine or improve your solution.

## DEFINE AND DELIMIT THE PROBLEM

When tackling an engineering challenge, the first step is to define the problem to be solved. To define the problem, you need to identify the characteristics that a solution must have to be successful. You can think of these characteristics as your criteria for success. You also need to identify any factors that might limit or restrict your solution. These limiting factors are the constraints on your design solution.

To take a simple example, perhaps you need a recipe to make a main dish for dinner. Your criteria for success might be that the dish tastes delicious and that it is nutritious. Some constraints might be that the ingredients cost less than $10 and that the recipe can be made in one hour or less. If any of the friends you'll be serving have food allergies, another constraint would be that the recipe not include any ingredients that would cause an allergic reaction.

In many cases, it is not possible to find a solution that meets all of the criteria perfectly while staying within the constraints. For that reason, you may find it helpful to prioritize your criteria so that you can identify the best tradeoffs between criteria and constraints. A useful tool for this purpose is a Pugh chart like the one on the next page.

## Lesson 3: Engineering Design Process *continued*

| CRITERIA | Maximum Value (1 to 5) | Solution A | Solution B | Solution C |
|---|---|---|---|---|
| | | | | |
| | | | | |
| | | | | |
| **Total Points** | | | | |
| | | | | |
| **CONSTRAINTS** | | | | |
| | Yes/No | | | |
| | Yes/No | | | |
| Which solution will you choose? Explain why. | | | | |

To use a Pugh chart to compare your solutions, follow these steps:

- List your criteria and constraints on the left side of the chart.
- List your possible solutions across the top.
- Prioritize your criteria by assigning a maximum value to each criterion, depending on how important it is.
- Rate each solution on how well it meets each criterion. If it meets the criterion perfectly, it gets the maximum value.
- Add up the points and indicate whether each solution meets all the constraints.

### Design Solutions

After you have identified your criteria and constraints, you are ready to brainstorm possible solutions. Often you will also need to research the problem and explore the possibilities. You may need to study the details of the problem or different aspects of the systems that are involved. You should also review the solutions and processes that people have developed for similar problems. It can be easier and less risky to adapt an existing solution than to invent a new solution. For example, it is usually easier to use or adapt a recipe than to invent one. Existing solutions have already been through cycles of optimization, so many of the component problems and issues have already been resolved. The effects of the solutions, including unintended consequences, are already known. You might be able to choose the best of several possible solutions, you might adjust one solution to suit your problem, or you might combine parts of different solutions.

Generate or find multiple solutions or approaches. Use your knowledge and your research to imagine possible solutions. The first idea is not necessarily the best idea, so try to ensure that you have explored a wide range of possibilities. Sometimes an unworkable idea can lead to a better idea. After you have generated a good set of ideas, use the criteria and constraints to evaluate the most promising ones. The use of criteria and constraints can help you be objective, especially when evaluating your own ideas.

Once you have selected the most promising solution, you will need to test it to determine how well it actually performs. The results of your testing help you to learn more about your materials and the design of your system. Sometimes you may choose to test more than one solution and then combine the strong points of each design into a new and better design solution.

## OPTIMIZE SOLUTIONS

You can use the results of your testing as feedback to refine and improve your solution. Some parts of your design may have worked well, while other parts were problematic. Focusing your attention on these problem areas will help you troubleshoot your design and come up with ideas for making it work better.

Testing, evaluating, and refining your solution should be an iterative process. That means you may repeat these steps in a series of design cycles to arrive at the best solution. These cycles of optimizing your solutions are often where the most important work takes place as you refine the details and make sure all the parts of your solution work together effectively.

## REFLECT AND COMMUNICATE

As with any process or skill, you will become better at engineering design as you practice it and gain more experience. Thinking reflectively about your design process is one of the best ways to improve. You may find it valuable to use a notebook to record notes about your design strategies and thinking as you work on developing a solution. Your notebook is also a place where you can make sketches and diagrams to explore your design ideas and to refine details of your design as you troubleshoot your solution.

The notes and sketches from your notebook can also be valuable resources when it comes time to communicate your design solution to others. The ability to communicate effectively is a valuable skill for engineers and other designers, who often need to explain and promote their solutions to customers or clients. They may also publish details of their design process in technical journals, so that other engineers can build on their work.

# Activity 1
# Design a Solar Car

In this activity, you will design, build, and test a model solar car.

## BACKGROUND

Concerns about the link between fossil fuel use and climate change, as well as the rapid depletion of nonrenewable energy sources, has increased interest in solar technology. A solar cell, also known as a photovoltaic cell, is a device that captures solar energy and converts it to electrical energy. Solar cells are made of two or more layers of silicon, a type of semiconductor. Small amounts of certain elements are added to each layer so that when the layers are side by side, an electric field develops across the cell. Sunlight provides the energy the electrons need to move across the cell. Wires attached to opposite layers of the solar cell can form a circuit so that the current can be used as a source of electrical energy.

The energy from a solar cell can be used to power an electric motor, which changes electrical energy to mechanical energy. A coil of wire inside the motor is on a shaft that can spin between opposite poles of a magnet. A current in the wire interacts with the magnetic field, rotating the coil and the shaft. This rotating shaft can be attached to gears or other devices, causing them to rotate as well.

### Materials

Use materials that your teacher provides or those of your choice.

### SAFETY

• Wear safety goggles, gloves, and an apron at all times.

• Handle sharp objects such as knives, scissors, and nails carefully.

## DESIGN CHALLENGE

**Objective:** Design, build, test, and modify a model solar-powered car that can transport a load.

Solar panels used as a source of electrical energy for homes and businesses are a common sight, but the use of solar cells for powering cars is still in the early stages of development. In this activity, you will investigate some of the obstacles to using solar-powered cars as you design, build, test, and modify a model solar-powered vehicle.

## DEFINE AND DELIMIT THE PROBLEM

Designing a full-sized car that operates almost exclusively on solar energy has proved to be challenging, even for experts. The most obvious problem is that solar cells require sunlight, and an energy storage system must be in place to deal with low- or no-light conditions. An energy storage system, however, can work only for a limited time. Efficiency of all systems in the car must therefore be

## Activity 1: Design a Solar Car *continued*

maximized in order to minimize power usage and allow the car to run as long as possible. Safety is also a concern for full-sized solar vehicles. Lightweight materials require less power to move, but the car may be susceptible to heavy damage during a collision.

Designing a model solar car is much simpler, but there are still many issues to consider. A model solar car can be designed to work only when the sun is bright, or if there is a way to store and use some of the energy later. Since your car will be carrying a load, the power generated by the system must be adequate to carry the full weight of the car and its load. Consider other factors, such as how big the car will be and the electrical system you will use. You will not yet outline specifically how the car will be constructed or the type of electrical parts you wish to include, but you need to have a general idea so that you can outline both cost and time constraints. Write a list of the criteria for your solar car and the constraints you anticipate in its design.

**Criteria and Constraints**

_____

_____

_____

_____

_____

_____

_____

_____

_____

_____

## DESIGN SOLUTIONS

Now that you've outlined the design challenge and listed criteria and constraints, you need to make decisions about how to construct your solar car. First, you need to decide how you want the electrical system to work. Think about the type of energy transfer you want to occur in your system and how you can design the system to accomplish that transfer. You also need to determine how to construct the body of the car. What parts will you include, and how will they merge with the electrical system to make your car run smoothly?

You might choose to start this process by brainstorming various design options with others in your group. Discuss benefits and possible drawbacks of each design. Look back at the list you made of criteria and constraints. Be sure any design specifications you consider adhere to the criteria and constraints. Research online for other design ideas, and discuss how you could implement parts of those designs into your solar car. Also research how a solar cell works and how a motor works. Decide how to arrange the electrical parts.

## Activity 1: Design a Solar Car *continued*

As part of your design, consider the parts that you will use for your car and the tools you will need for construction. A solar cell captures energy from the sun, but you need to have components in your electrical system that transform that energy in order to move your car. You will need a gear system between the motor and the front or rear axle of your car to turn the wheels. Think about how you will start and stop the car. Also consider how you will keep the parts of the electrical system and the load stable while the car is moving.

Sketch the design of the electrical system of your solar car in the space below. Be sure to label all components and show how they will be connected. Then make a separate sketch of the car, showing how all of the parts will work together.

**Design Sketch—Electrical System**

**Design Sketch—Model Solar Car**

**Activity 1: Design a Solar Car** *continued*

## OPTIMIZE YOUR SOLUTION

After you have constructed your model solar car, it's time to test its performance. Your teacher will designate a place and time for the tests. Once again, look back at the criteria you listed for successful performance of the model solar car. Take careful notes about your car's performance. Observations might include how fast the car starts, the speed of the car as it carries various loads, and how well it travels along a straight path. If you have included an energy storage component in the electrical system, test how well the car performs as the car travels into a shaded area.

Based on your notes, decide how you can improve your car's performance. A car that turns, for example, may need an adjustment to its wheel-and-axle system. An important part of optimizing your car's performance is considering its electrical system. Use a multimeter to measure the voltage and current, and based on these values, calculate the power output. Consider how you might increase the power by making changes to your car. For example, you could try changing the solar cell or the motor, or you might change the wiring in some way. Make new measurements after each change to test its effect. Afterwards, make new observations of the car's speed. Carefully record the results of each test so you can understand which changes were effective and which were not.

Continue to modify and test your solar car until you are satisfied with its performance. In the space below, record all of your modifications and test results. Be sure to include both successful and unsuccessful results. Explain how your design meets the criteria you set for your model solar car.

### Test Results

_____

_____

_____

_____

_____

_____

_____

_____

_____

_____

| Activity 1: Design a Solar Car *continued*

Answer the following questions about your model solar car and its tests.

1. Compare the original version of your solar car with the version after your testing and modifications. Explain why you did or did not choose to modify your car.

   _____

   _____

   _____

   _____

   _____

2. Explain the energy transfer that occurs in your car and how conservation of energy relates to the function of your solar car.

   _____

   _____

   _____

   _____

   _____

3. Vehicles that run primarily on solar energy are not available for everyday use. Based on your research and observations, what obstacles do you think this technology must still overcome before it can be widely used?

   _____

   _____

   _____

   _____

   _____

   _____

**Activity 1: Design a Solar Car** *continued*

## EXTENSION

One of the challenges you probably faced in the design and testing of your solar car was balancing speed and power. Increasing the load that the car carries decreases its speed, but more power is required to increase the speed. Test the speed of your solar car by racing against solar cars built by other groups in your class. Each car should carry the same load and move along parallel tracks to ensure that the sunlight received by each car is the same. Afterwards, discuss how the design of each car contributed to its performance in the race.

# Activity 2
# Design a Patient-Transport Device

In this activity, you will design, build, test, and revise models of patient transport devices.

## BACKGROUND

Safety is always a concern while driving or riding in a vehicle. Seat belts, airbags, antilock brakes, traction control, accident avoidance systems, and many other features all contribute to a safer ride. However, accidents sometimes happen, and of the many types of collisions that are possible, most of which are dangerous, the head-on collision involves the greatest forces. The safety features engineers have designed into vehicles increase the chances that both the driver and the passengers will survive the crash.

However, what if the vehicle in question is an ambulance speeding down the highway? What if the passengers include a patient lying down in the back of the vehicle? In this situation, the patient is secured to a patient transport device, such as a gurney used to move the patient in and out of the ambulance. The crew in the back of the ambulance provides medical care to the patient while the ambulance is moving above the normal speed limit en route to the hospital. What additional and unique safety concerns are there, particularly for the patient, if the ambulance is involved in a head-on collision?

### Materials

Use materials that your teacher provides or those of your choice.

### SAFETY

- Wear safety goggles and an apron at all times.
- Handle sharp objects such as knives, scissors, and tin snips carefully.
- Clean up any spills quickly. Wash your hands if you've handled broken eggs.

## DESIGN CHALLENGE

**Objective:** Design, build, test, and revise a model of a patient-transport device that can be used in an ambulance and can withstand a head-on collision.

The severity of a head-on collision is determined in part by the speed at which the vehicles are traveling. For simplicity, you will crash your model into a solid barrier—a wall—so that your concern is the speed of the model and not of another vehicle. To gauge the effectiveness of your device, you will incrementally increase the speed at which the device travels. The greater the speed is at which your patient survives, the more effective is your device. Your team's challenge is to design, construct, test, and revise your model to increase the effectiveness of the device to give your patient the best change for survival in a crash. The model for your patient will be a raw egg.

| Activity 2: Design a Patient-Transport Device *continued*

## DEFINE AND DELIMIT THE PROBLEM

You will build a model of a patient-transport device for your egg "patient" and then attach that device to a simple model ambulance. Research how patients are transported to a hospital in an emergency. Focus on the patient-transport device (gurney) to which the patient is secured and on which the patient is transported into and out of the ambulance.

Always keep in mind the function of the patient-transport device. Consider how the device will be secured to the ambulance, knowing that the device has to be easily and quickly removable. Think about how you will secure the patient to the transport device. The restraints cannot completely enclose the patient, because the device has to allow the crew access to the patient for treatment while in transit.

Consider the dimensions and mass of the device you will build. It cannot occupy the entire ambulance, because room is needed in the front for the driver and in the back compartment for the crew. The more mass it contains, the more kinetic energy the entire assembly will have during a crash and the more severe the crash may be.

Consider also the materials you will use for your model and their cost and availability. Then write a list of the criteria and constraints for your design.

**Criteria and Constraints**

_____

_____

_____

_____

_____

_____

_____

_____

_____

## DESIGN SOLUTIONS

Now you will need to make decisions about how to construct and test your patient-transport device, as well as the area in which you will test it. One option for controlling the speed of your model ambulance and patient-transport device assembly is to use a ramp, which can be raised after each run to incrementally increase the speed of the model. If the patient "survives"—that is, if the egg is not at all damaged—at the lowest speed, then increase the speed of the model by increasing the height of the ramp.

When you have chosen a design for your patient-transport device and the design of your testing setup, sketch both in the spaces on the next page. Decide on the best procedures to follow. Then build your model and the testing setup.

## Activity 2: Design a Patient-Transport Device *continued*

**Design Sketch—Patient-Transport Device and Ambulance**

**Design Sketch—Testing Setup**

## OPTIMIZE YOUR SOLUTION

After you have constructed your model, it's time to test its performance. Your teacher will designate a place and time for the tests. Once again, look back at the criteria you listed for successful performance of your model.

Take careful notes about the model's performance during each of its runs. Test your model at the slowest speed first. If the model successfully passes the test at this speed, move up to the next higher speed for the next run. Continue to test at increasingly higher speeds until the model fails or until you've reached the highest speed for your test setup. Data to record for each run might include the height of the ramp (if used), the speed of the model, and the mass of the device. Observations might include descriptions or sketches of the device before and after the impact with the wall. In the table on the next page, record data and observations for each run.

**Activity 2: Design a Patient-Transport Device** *continued*

In the Notes section, record where and how any failures occurred, either in the model or the test setup. Based on your notes and observations, describe any changes you might make to improve the model or the test setup or to trade less important features for those that are more important. Decide which changes you want to make, and then implement those changes and retest your modified model. Be sure to record all data associated with the modification. Finally, explain how your design addresses the problem you are trying to solve.

**Test Results**

| Test Run | Data | Observations |
|---|---|---|
| 1 | | |
| 2 | | |
| 3 | | |
| 4 | | |
| 5 | | |

**Notes on Test**

_____

_____

_____

_____

_____

_____

_____

## Activity 2: Design a Patient-Transport Device *continued*

Answer the following questions about your model and its test.

1. Compare the original version of your patient transport device with the version after your modifications. Explain why you chose to modify your device.

_____

_____

_____

_____

_____

**2.** Which criteria did you find most difficult to meet?

_____

_____

_____

_____

_____

## EXTENSION

In real life, when ambulances are driving through traffic in an emergency, vehicles and hazards are all around, and collisions are not always strictly head-on. A good design for a patient-transport device should be able to help a patient survive in as many different crash scenarios as possible. Design an experiment to test collisions in different directions, such as a side-on collision and a rear-end collision. Test variations on the speed of the crash. When conducting these experiments, be sure you are changing only one variable at a time. With teacher approval, perform your tests using appropriate safety measures. Share your results with the class.

# Activity 3
# Design a Passive Solar House

In this activity, you will design and construct a model house that uses various methods of passive solar heating to convert solar energy to thermal energy.

## BACKGROUND

The impact of global climate change and its link to fossil fuel use has led to an increased interest in renewable energy, including solar energy. Using energy from the sun as a means of heating homes makes sense, even during cold winter months, but careful design choices must be made to use solar heating effectively.

Passive solar heating uses no electricity and no mechanical devices to heat a home. The building must therefore be carefully designed to use sunlight for heating in the winter and block or reflect sunlight in the summer. For homes in the mid-northern latitudes, the midday sun is always located in the southern sky, but it is much higher in the sky in summer than in winter. A home designed for solar heating will have windows positioned to take advantage of the sunlight in the winter and a method of blocking sunlight that strikes windows in the summer.

Another aspect of passive solar heating involves choosing appropriate materials for constructing a home. The color of materials is one factor because a dark-colored surface absorbs most of the light that strikes it, and the increased energy heats the surface. A light-colored surface reflects most of the light, so the surface tends to be cooler. Thermal mass is a property of a material that enables it to absorb and store thermal energy. Materials such as rock, tile, and concrete have a high thermal mass. These materials are useful in a home because they absorb energy from the sun during the day and slowly release the energy to warm a room at night. Insulating materials placed inside walls can hinder heat transfer into or out of a room. Foam, for example, is a good thermal insulator.

Airflow also affects the temperature of a passive solar house. Placement of windows and ceiling height affect the flow of air within a building. In summer, air flowing through windows from one side of a house to the other can keep the house cooler.

## Materials

Use materials that your teacher provides or those of your choice.

## SAFETY

• Wear safety goggles at all times.

• Handle sharp objects such as knives, scissors, and nails carefully.

• Be careful not to touch the hot bulb of a lamp.

**Activity 3: Design a Passive Solar House** *continued*

## DESIGN CHALLENGE

**Objective:** Design, build, test, and modify a one-story model house that uses passive solar heating.

Your model house must include the following features:

- a floor area of at least 400 cm$^2$
- a roof at least 12 cm high
- no interior walls
- exterior walls no thicker than 3 cm
- no highly reflective materials (such as foil) on exterior walls
- at least two reasonably sized windows
- a reasonably sized door
- a small hole in the roof through which a thermometer can be placed (The thermometer should be readable through a window.)

After you construct your model house, you will test it in one situation that simulates a hot summer day and another situation that simulates a cold winter day.

## DEFINE AND DELIMIT THE PROBLEM

Research various methods of passive solar heating. Then apply what you have learned to your design challenge. What problems do you need to solve? What factors do you need to consider when designing the model? You have been provided with some constraints on your model house, but what other constraints do you think the design will have?

Write a list of the criteria for your model house and the constraints you anticipate in its design. As you do, consider how your model house will minimize heating in summer and maximize heating in winter. Consider also whether the cost of the design would be reasonable for real-world applications and whether homebuyers would likely purchase a home with the design features you have chosen.

**Criteria and Constraints**

_____

_____

_____

_____

_____

_____

_____

_____

_____

_____

Activity 3: Design a Passive Solar House *continued*

## DESIGN SOLUTIONS

Using the criteria and constraints that you have identified, you now need to make decisions about the design of your model house. Conduct further research of passive solar heating designs if necessary. Then sketch a floor plan for your house. What size will it be? How thick will the walls be? What materials will you use for the construction of the floor?

Next, draw one or more side views of your model house. Show the placement and sizes of the windows and the door. Indicate the materials you will use for the walls. Show what the roof will look like, and label the material you will use to construct it.

**Design Sketch—Floor Plan**

**Design Sketch—Side View(s) and Roof Design**

| Activity 3: Design a Passive Solar House *continued* |

## OPTIMIZE YOUR SOLUTION

After you construct your model home, it's time to see how well it uses passive solar heating. You will have two opportunities to test your model. Each test will have two parts: Part 1 will test the change in temperature inside your model home during an 8-minute period for a simulated hot summer day. Part 2 will test the change in temperature inside your model home during an 8-minute period for a simulated cold winter day. After the first two-part test, you will have an opportunity to modify your model based on the data collected.

Record the temperature measurements for each set of tests below. Make a temperature vs. time graph for each set of data. Also write a description of modifications that you made to your model house. For each modification that you make, explain how you expect the change to improve the model's performance.

### Test 1 Data

| | Summer Day | | | Winter Day | |
|---|---|---|---|---|---|
| Time (min) | Temperature (°C) | | Time (min) | Temperature (°C) |
| 0.0 | | | 0.0 | |
| 0.5 | | | 0.5 | |
| 1.0 | | | 1.0 | |
| 1.5 | | | 1.5 | |
| 2.0 | | | 2.0 | |
| 2.5 | | | 2.5 | |
| 3.0 | | | 3.0 | |
| 3.5 | | | 3.5 | |
| 4.0 | | | 4.0 | |
| 4.5 | | | 4.5 | |
| 5.0 | | | 5.0 | |
| 5.5 | | | 5.5 | |
| 6.0 | | | 6.0 | |
| 6.5 | | | 6.5 | |
| 7.0 | | | 7.0 | |
| 7.5 | | | 7.5 | |
| 8.0 | | | 8.0 | |

| Activity 3: Design a Passive Solar House *continued*

## Graph

## Test 1 Results and Modifications

_____

_____

_____

_____

_____

_____

_____

_____

_____

_____

_____

_____

_____

_____

Activity 3: Design a Passive Solar House *continued*

**Test 2 Data**

| Summer Day | | | Winter Day | |
|---|---|---|---|---|
| Time (min) | Temperature (°C) | | Time (min) | Temperature (°C) |
| 0.0 | | | 0.0 | |
| 0.5 | | | 0.5 | |
| 1.0 | | | 1.0 | |
| 1.5 | | | 1.5 | |
| 2.0 | | | 2.0 | |
| 2.5 | | | 2.5 | |
| 3.0 | | | 3.0 | |
| 3.5 | | | 3.5 | |
| 4.0 | | | 4.0 | |
| 4.5 | | | 4.5 | |
| 5.0 | | | 5.0 | |
| 5.5 | | | 5.5 | |
| 6.0 | | | 6.0 | |
| 6.5 | | | 6.5 | |
| 7.0 | | | 7.0 | |
| 7.5 | | | 7.5 | |
| 8.0 | | | 8.0 | |

**Graph**

Name _____ Class _____ Date _____

Answer the following questions about your model house design and its tests.

1. Summarize the design criteria that you incorporated into the first version of your model house so that it could use passive solar heating to keep the house warm in winter yet stay cool in summer.

_____

_____

_____

_____

_____

_____

2. Were the modifications that you made after the first test of your model house effective? Explain why or why not.

_____

_____

_____

_____

_____

_____

3. How are the passive solar heating design features that you used for your model house similar to or different from methods used in a real house? What are some features you would use in a real house design that you were unable to use in your model house? Explain the benefits of these features.

_____

_____

_____

_____

_____

_____

_____

**Activity 3: Design a Passive Solar House** *continued*

## EXTENSION

Using passive solar heating for a home requires more than just using solar energy to heat the home in the winter and using the design of the building to block heat in the summer. Homes must also be able to retain the thermal energy they gain from sunlight on winter days and slowly release it to warm the home throughout winter nights. Homes might use outdoor vegetation to reduce solar heating of the home in the summer, but this vegetation should not block sunlight from reaching the home in the winter. Modify your model house's design to address these needs. Then design and carry out a test of your modifications.

# Activity 4
# Design a Solution Using a
# Piezoelectric Generator

In this activity, you will identify a real-world problem and design a solution that incorporates piezoelectric technology.

## BACKGROUND

Think about energy you use when running, lifting a backpack, or putting on a coat. Part of the energy you use goes into the ground, the backpack, or the coat. Imagine if you could capture this energy and use it for other purposes, such as powering a cell phone or a lamp. Energy harvesting is a method of capturing and using such energy that is otherwise unused. The need for worldwide energy conservation has initiated investigations into how energy harvesting can be applied to power modern technology. One type of energy harvesting is the use of electronic circuits that respond to forces and vibrations. In this activity, you will identify a real-world problem that can be solved by incorporating this type of energy-harvesting circuit.

   A piezoelectric material is a crystalline substance that generates voltage when subjected to a force or vibration. A crystal is any solid in which the particles have a repeating, geometric arrangement. In a piezoelectric crystal, the particles are arranged so that the balanced charge in the crystal structure is disturbed when the crystal is squeezed or stretched, producing a net charge on each side of the crystal. The sign of the charges reverses if the crystal is compressed and then stretched. A piezoelectric material therefore transforms mechanical energy from applied force into electrical energy. When placed in an electrical circuit, piezoelectric materials can be used to harvest the energy of forces exerted on the material.

### Materials

Use materials that your teacher provides or those of your choice.

### SAFETY

- Wear safety goggles at all times.
- Never close a circuit until your teacher has approved it.
- To avoid a shock, be careful not to touch wiring while the capacitor is charging. Always discharge the capacitor.

## DESIGN CHALLENGE

**Objective:** Identify a real-world problem and design a solution that incorporates piezoelectric technology.

Activity 4: Design a Solution Using a Piezoelectric Generator *continued*

All around you, mechanical energy that could be used to power electrical devices is lost to the environment. Engineers have been developing ways to harvest this energy for useful purposes. You will start this activity by creating a piezoelectric circuit and observing how it works. Using what you learn, you will then identify a real-world problem that can be solved by harvesting mechanical energy using a piezoelectric generator to run an electrical device.

## CREATE A PIEZOELECTRIC CIRCUIT

To help you understand piezoelectricity, your teacher will guide you in constructing a piezoelectric circuit on a breadboard, a base for prototyping electronics. The following list describes some of the components you will use in your circuit:

- A *piezo element* is a thin slice of piezoelectric material surrounded by a metal disk. Wire leads are attached to the disk. When you tap the disk, the piezoelectric material responds by generating a voltage.

- A *capacitor* is an electrical component that stores electrical potential energy.

- A *diode* is an electrical component that allows an electrical charge to move in only one direction across it.

- A *diode bridge* is an arrangement of at least four diodes in a circuit that changes alternating current (AC) into direct current (DC).

- A *light-emitting diode (LED)* is a diode that gives off light when a current flows through it.

- A *toggle switch* is an electrical component that can switch the path of current. In your circuit, flipping the switch one way will charge the capacitor and flipping it the other way will power the LED.

Your teacher will demonstrate the following steps you should take to create your circuit:

1. Make a diode bridge on the breadboard: Connect diodes from 5A to 8A, from 5B to 10B, from 8C to 13C, and from 10A to 13A.

2. Connect the negative lead of the piezo element to 8E and the positive lead to 10E.

3. Connect the positive lead of the capacitor to 13E and the negative lead to 13G.

4. For the toggle switch, insert the middle lead to 13J and the other leads to 5E and 21E.

5. Connect the positive lead of the LED to 24A and the negative lead to 21A.

Have your teacher check your completed circuit. Then begin tapping the piezo element to provide voltage to the circuit. If the LED briefly blinks on, the current is being discharged through the LED. If the LED does not blink on, then the current is being used to charge the capacitor. Your teacher will demonstrate how to connect the multimeter to your circuit to monitor the charging of the capacitor. Once the capacitor is sufficiently charged, you can flip the toggle switch and the LED will light up briefly as the capacitor discharges, even though you are not tapping the piezo element.

| Activity 4: Design a Solution Using a Piezoelectric Generator *continued* |

## DEFINE AND DELIMIT THE PROBLEM

Now that you have experience working with a piezoelectric circuit, you will consider how to apply this technology to solve a real-world problem. Research online to learn about the importance of energy harvesting and why piezoelectric generators can be used for this purpose. Identify a problem that can be solved by harvesting energy using a piezoelectric generator. Think about the criteria and constraints that such a system would have.

The piezoelectric materials used for real-life applications of energy harvesting are often engineered to increase voltage and make the materials a better fit for the application. Constraints also apply to the piezo element you use. Think about what you learned from using the piezo element to power an LED and how the constraints identified in that circuit apply to the electrical device you will use. Consider the following questions:

- What are the constraints on the electrical devices that would be powered by the application you have identified?

- How much time would be required to design, build, and test the system you are proposing?

- How much would the materials cost to construct the system?

List the criteria and constraints of your proposed system below.

### Criteria and Constraints

_____

_____

_____

_____

_____

_____

_____

## DESIGN SOLUTIONS

Describe a design solution that could be used to solve the problem you have identified. Explain the role that a piezoelectric circuit would have in your design. Determine and describe how the circuit would harvest mechanical energy with a piezoelectric generator. Think about how energy will be transferred in your system. What will be the source of mechanical energy? How will this energy be changed to electrical energy? Consider the constraints you have identified and how they will affect your design.

Write your descriptions, explanations, and notes below. Then draw and label a sketch of your proposed energy-harvesting system on the next page. Be sure to label all components and show how they will be connected.

**Activity 4: Design a Solution Using a Piezoelectric Generator** *continued*

_____

_____

_____

_____

_____

_____

_____

_____

_____

_____

_____

## Design Sketch—Piezoelectric Energy-Harvesting System

Activity 4: Design a Solution Using a Piezoelectric Generator *continued*

## OPTIMIZE YOUR SOLUTION

Consider how you could implement modifications to the piezoelectric circuit design to improve the energy-harvesting capabilities of the circuit in your system. Think about the way in which electrical energy is transferred through your circuit. What changes could you make to improve the energy transfer in the circuit design? Could you add more of any of the existing components? If so, should they be included in parallel or in series? For example, could you add one or more additional piezo elements? Could you add one or more additional capacitors? Should a resistor be inserted? Discuss with your team the effect that each of these changes might have. Could you increase the input of mechanical energy? In general, think about how you could increase the amount of energy that you harvest with your piezo system. You may need to conduct research to investigate the circuit design and to get ideas for your system improvements. Brainstorm various design options with your team. Then describe your proposed circuit adaptations below.

_____

_____

_____

_____

_____

_____

_____

_____

Answer the following questions about your piezoelectric energy-harvesting system and the adaptations that you propose for the circuit design.

1. Describe how the system you designed could be useful in everyday life. Explain the energy transformations and transfer that would occur in the system if it were constructed.

_____

_____

_____

_____

## Activity 4: Design a Solution Using a Piezoelectric Generator *continued*

**2.** What are piezoelectric materials? Why are they useful for harvesting energy from the surroundings?

_____

_____

_____

_____

**3.** Explain difficulties that might have to be overcome in implementing your piezoelectric system in a real-life situation.

_____

_____

_____

_____

_____

**4.** Why do you think there is increased interest in developing piezoelectric energy-harvesting systems?

_____

_____

_____

_____

## EXTENSION

Create a slideshow describing your ideas for using piezoelectric energy harvesting to solve a real-world problem, and present your slideshow to your class. After all groups have presented their ideas, debate your design solutions with your classmates.

# Activity 5
# Design a System to Estimate
# Information Storage Capacity

In this activity, you will design, test, and modify a system to estimate the storage capacity of a CD and a DVD.

## BACKGROUND

One of the challenges of our high-tech world is to store increasing amounts of information in compact, easily accessible ways. Optical storage discs, such as CDs, DVDs, and Blu-ray Discs™, use lasers to read and write digital information. One of the primary differences in the types of discs is their storage capacity. How can you estimate the storage capacity of an optical disc?

Information is stored on an optical disc as a series of indentations, called *pits,* with flat spaces between them, called *lands*. A track of pits and lands spirals from the center of the disc toward the edge. Information is encoded in the pattern of pits and lands. As a disc rotates, laser light moves along the track, and its reflection sends information about the encoded pattern to a sensor. *Pitch* is the distance between rows of a disc's spiral track. It is a good indication of a disc's information storage capacity.

CDs have the lowest storage capacity because they have the greatest pitch. The large pitch means long-wavelength red laser light can be used to read the pattern of pits and lands on a CD. Blu-ray Discs have the smallest pitch. The small pitch means short-wavelength blue laser light must be used with a Blu-ray Disc. A DVD's pitch is between that of a CD and a Blu-ray Disc.

If you hold an optical disc near light, you see a rainbow of colors on its surface. The rows of the spiral track on the disc act like a diffraction grating to disperse light into different wavelengths by constructive interference. If you shine a laser perpendicularly toward the disc, beams of light reflect at certain angles, $\theta$, that you can measure. If you know the wavelength, $\lambda$, of the laser light, you can use the constructive interference equation, $d\sin\theta = \pm m\lambda$, to calculate $d$, the pitch of the disc. The variable $m = 0, 1, 2, 3, \ldots$ is the number of the reflected beam. The pitch and the estimates of the number of pits on a track allow you to approximate the storage capacity of the disc.

### Materials

Use materials that your teacher provides or those of your choice.

### SAFETY

• Wear safety goggles at all times.

• Be careful not to look directly at laser light or shine it toward anyone's eyes.

Blu-ray Disc™ is a trademark of the Blu-ray Disc Association.

| Activity 5: Design a System to Estimate Information Storage Capacity *continued*

## DESIGN CHALLENGE

**Objective:** Design an experiment to estimate the pitch of optical media.

## DEFINE AND DELIMIT THE PROBLEM

Before you design the system that you will use to estimate the storage capacity of a disc, discuss with your team the goals and limitations of your investigation. How closely do you feel your estimate of the storage capacity should be to the actual value in order for your design to be successful? What are reasonable measurements that your design system should obtain that would indicate that you have a good design? You may need to do research to determine certain reasonable criteria for the optical discs that you will investigate. Write a list of the criteria for your system and constraints you anticipate in its design.

### Criteria and Constraints

_____

_____

_____

_____

_____

_____

_____

_____

_____

## DESIGN SOLUTIONS

Using the criteria and constraints that you have identified, make decisions about the design of the system you will use to estimate the storage capacity of a disc. Start by sketching the layout of the materials. Where will the laser pointer be positioned? How will you orient the optical discs? What measurements will you make? As you make these decisions, keep in mind the calculations you will eventually have to make to estimate the storage capacity of the disc.

The primary factor that you will be able to measure is the diffraction angle. You will then use this angle in the diffraction equation to calculate the pitch and estimate the storage capacity. How will your design enable you to make this measurement using diffraction of the laser light? Be sure to label all parts of the layout that you sketch.

Name _____ Class _____ Date _____

**Design Sketch**

```


```

## OPTIMIZE YOUR SOLUTION

Once you have completed the initial design of your system, discuss your setup
with your team. What do you think will work well? What might be problematic?
Based on your discussion, modify your design and draw a revised design sketch.

**Modified Design Sketch**

```


```

**Activity 5: Design a System to Estimate Information Storage Capacity** *continued*

## Modifications

Describe the modifications you made to your design.

_____

_____

_____

_____

_____

_____

_____

## TEST YOUR DESIGN

Now it's time to test your design. Measure the diffraction angle of the CD and DVD, and calculate the pitch. Then use your results along with any necessary calculations to again estimate the storage capacity of each disc.

Diffraction angle of CD: _____          Diffraction angle of DVD: _____

## Test Calculations

| **Activity 5: Design a System to Estimate Information Storage Capacity** *continued* |

Answer the following questions about the design of your system, your measurements, and your results.

1. Do you think your team designed and constructed a system that was able to reasonably estimate the storage capacity of a CD and a DVD? Explain what you think was or was not successful about your design.

_____

_____

_____

_____

_____

2. Explain what you hoped to achieve with the modifications you made to your design. Do you think the modifications made a significant difference? Why or why not?

_____

_____

_____

_____

_____

3. Work with your team to design a way to store even more data on an optical disc. Describe changes you would make and how those changes would enable more information to be encoded on the disc. What effects do you think the changes would have on the cost and reliability of a disc?

_____

_____

_____

_____

_____

**EXTENSION**

Create a computer slideshow presentation explaining your experimental design, your measurements, and your calculations. Share your presentation with the class